Long.Beach, Ca.

Front cover ukulele photo courtesy of Flight Instruments

ISBN 978-1-70514-018-5

HAL•LEONARD®

Visit Hal Leonard Online at
www.halleonard.com

World headquarters, contact:
Hal Leonard
7777 West Bluemound Road
Milwaukee, WI 53213
Email: info@halleonard.com

In Europe, contact:
Hal Leonard Europe Limited
42 Wigmore Street
Marylebone, London, W1U 2RY
Email: info@halleonardeurope.com

In Australia, contact:
Hal Leonard Australia Pty. Ltd.
4 Lentara Court
Cheltenham, Victoria, 3192 Australia
Email: info@halleonard.com.au

CONTENTS

4 April 29, 1992 (Miami)

13 Badfish

16 Boss D.J.

21 Caress Me Down

28 Date Rape

46 Doin' Time

37 Don't Push

52 Garden Grove

56 Jailhouse

60 Let's Go Get Stoned

64 Same in the End

72 Santeria

76 Scarlet Begonias

69 Smoke Two Joints

86 What I Got

81 Wrong Way

April 29, 1992

(Miami)

Words and Music by Brad Nowell, Lawrence Krsone Parker, Marshall Goodman and Mike Happoldt

First note

Intro
Moderately

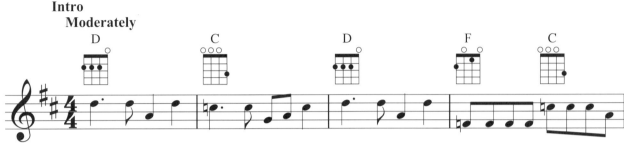

Police Chatter 1: See additional lyrics

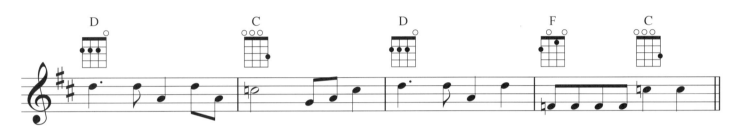

Verse

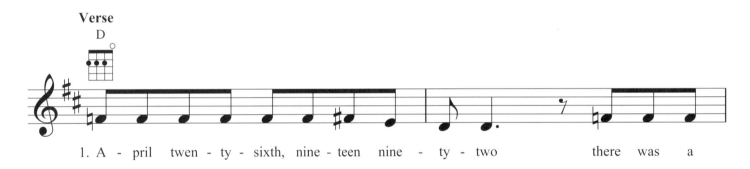

1. A - pril twen - ty - sixth, nine - teen nine - ty - two there was a

ri - ot on the streets. Tell me, where were you?

You were sit - ting home watch - ing your T - V while I was

par - tic - i - pat - ing in some an - ar - chy. First spot we hit, it was my

liq - uor store. I fi - nal - ly got all that al - co - hol I can't af - ford. With

red lights flash - ing, time _____ to re - tire, _____ and then we

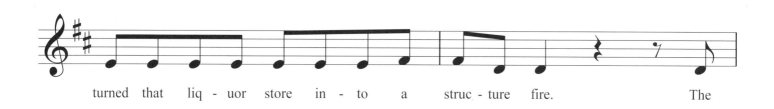

turned that liq - uor store in - to a struc - ture fire. The

next stop we hit, it was the mu - sic shop. It on - ly

took one brick to make that win - dow drop. Fi - nal - ly we got our own __

_____ P. A.   Where do you think I got this gui-tar that you're

Interlude
N.C.
Play 3 times

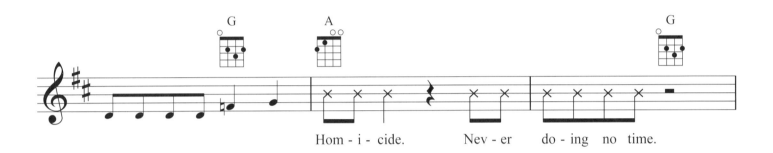

hear-ing to-day? ___   *Police Chatter 2: See additional lyrics*

Hom - i - cide.   Nev - er   do - ing no time.

Verse

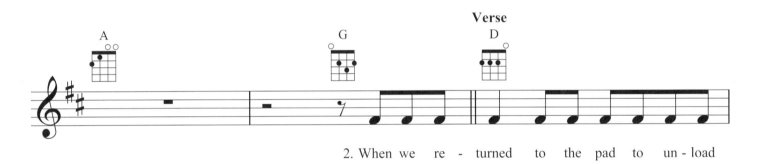

2. When we re - turned   to the pad to un - load

ev - 'ry - thing,   it   dawned on me that I need new home

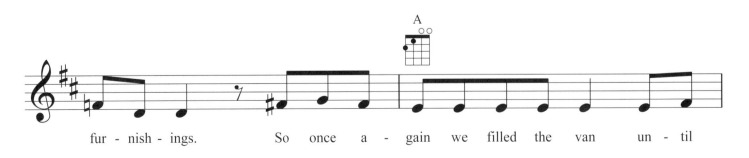

fur - nish - ings.   So once a - gain we filled the van un - til

it was full.   Since that day, my liv - ing room's been much more

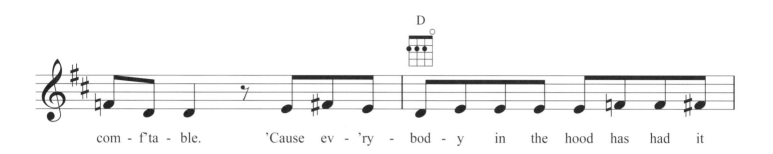

com - f'ta - ble.   'Cause ev - 'ry - bod - y in the hood has had it

up to here.   It's get - ting hot - ter and hot - ter, and hard - er

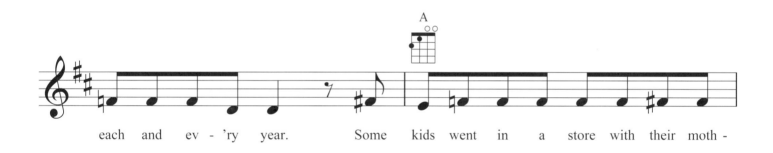

each and ev - 'ry year.   Some kids went in a store with their moth -

er.   I saw her when she came out; she was

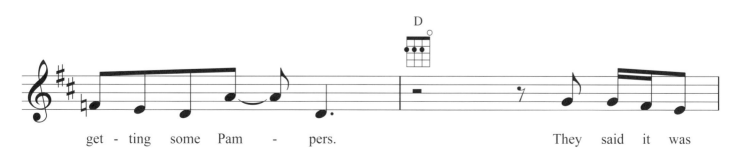

get - ting some Pam - pers.   They said it was

for the black man, they said it was for the Mex - i - can, and

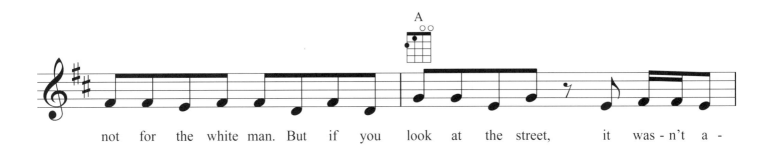

not for the white man. But if you look at the street, it was - n't a -

bout Rod - ney King and this fucked - up sit - u - a - tion and these

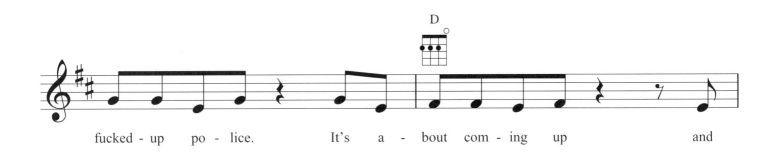

fucked - up po - lice. It's a - bout com - ing up and

stay - ing on top and scream - ing, "One - eight - sev - en on a

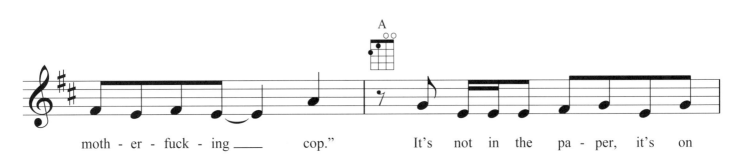

moth - er - fuck - ing ___ cop." It's not in the pa - per, it's on

the wall.　　Na - tion - al　Guard,　　　　　smoke　from　all　a - round.

Interlude

N.C.

Play 4 times

D

Police Chatter 3: See additional lyrics

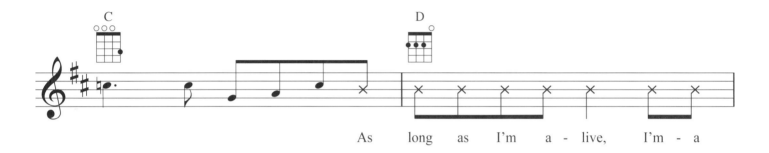

C　　　　　　　　　　　　　D

As　　long　as　I'm　a - live,　　I'm　a

Bridge

F　　　　C　　　　　D

live　il - le - gal.　　　Let　it　burn,　　wan - na　let　it　burn,

wan - na　let　it　burn,　wan - na,　wan - na　let　it　burn. _____

A

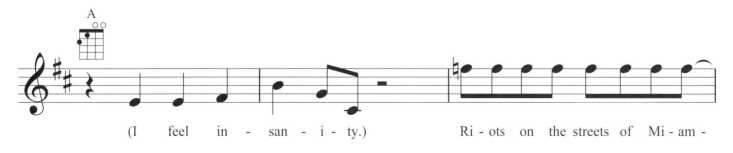

(I　feel　in - san - i - ty.)　　Ri - ots　on　the　streets　of　Mi - am -

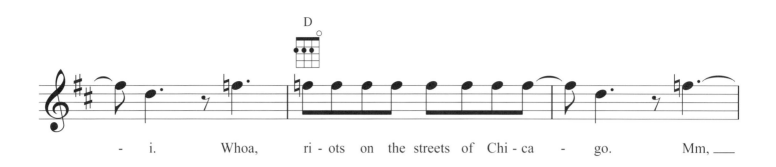

- i. Whoa, ri - ots on the streets of Chi - ca - go. Mm, ___

___ on the streets of Long ___ Beach. Mm,

in San Fran - cis - co.
(I feel in - san - i - ty.)

Ri - ots on the streets of Kan - sas Cit - y. Oh,

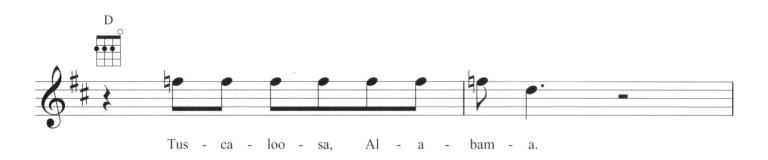

Tus - ca - loo - sa, Al - a - bam - a.

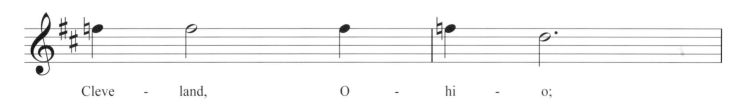

Cleve - land, O - hi - o;

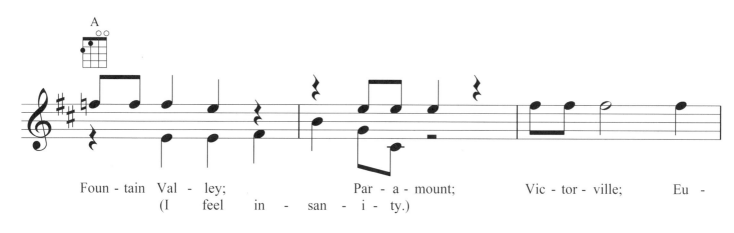

Foun - tain Val - ley; Par - a - mount; Vic - tor - ville; Eu -
(I   feel   in - san - i - ty.)

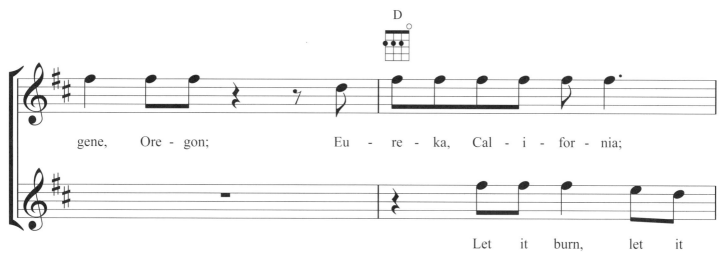

gene, Ore - gon; Eu - re - ka, Cal - i - for - nia;

Let   it   burn,   let   it

Hes - per - i - a; San - ta Bar -

burn,   let   it   burn. Won't you let it burn? Won't you,

- b'ra; Cu - ya - ma - ca, Ne - vad - a; Phoe - nix, Ar - i - zo - na;

won't you let it burn? _____   Let   it   burn. _____

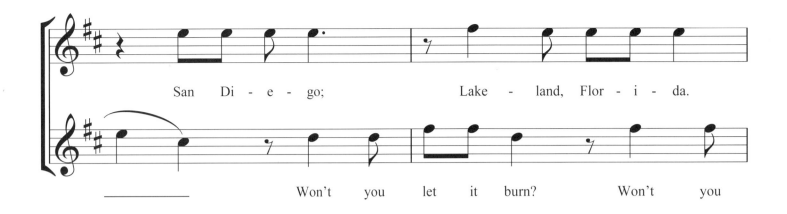

San Di - e - go; Lake - land, Flor - i - da.

_____ Won't you let it burn? Won't you

Outro

N.C.

Fuck - in' Twen - ty - nine Palms. *Police Chatter 4: See additional lyrics*

let it burn? _____ Let it burn. _____
(Vocal 1st time only)

Play 3 times

Additional Lyrics

1. "I don't know if you can, but can you get an owner for ONS, that's O-N-S, Junior Market?
The address is nineteen thirty-four East Anaheim. All the windows are busted out, and it's like a free-for-all in here.
And, uh, the owner should maybe come down here and see if he can secure his business, if he wants to."

2. "Call Fire and tell their units to respond at a Mobil station, Alamitos and Anaheim.
It's, uh, flaming up good."
"Ten-four, Alamitos and Anaheim."

3. "Units, units be advised, there is an attempt to arrest now at nine-three-eight Temple, nine-three-eight Temple.
Thirty subjects with bats trying to get inside the CP's house.
He thinks they're gonna start, they're trying to kill him."

4. "Ten-four. Any units assist, Frank seventy-four Willow at Caspian.
Structure fire and... numerous subjects looting."
"Ten fifteen to get rid of this looter."
"Ten four."

Badfish

Words and Music by Brad Nowell

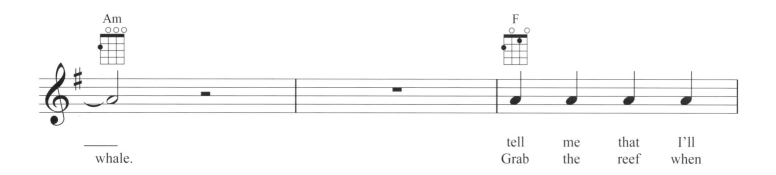

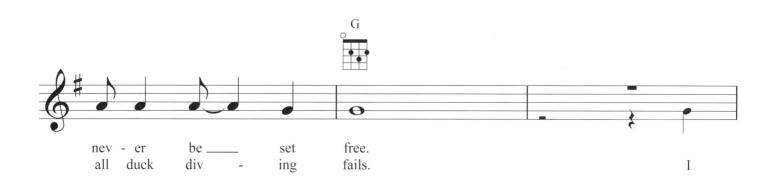

Creep and crawl, I step in - to _____ the
The wa - ter's too pol - lut - ed _____ with

night.
germs.   I dive deep   Two   when it's

pints   of   booze. _____
ten   feet   o - ver - head, _____

Tell me: are   you   a bad - fish,   too?
grab _ the reef   un - der - neath _ my   bed.

%: Chorus

Ain't   got   no   mon - ey   to   spend. ___
Ain't   got   no   quar - rels   with   God. ___
Ain't   got   no   quar - rels   with   God. ___

_____   I   hope   the
_____   Ain't   got   no
_____   Ain't   got   no

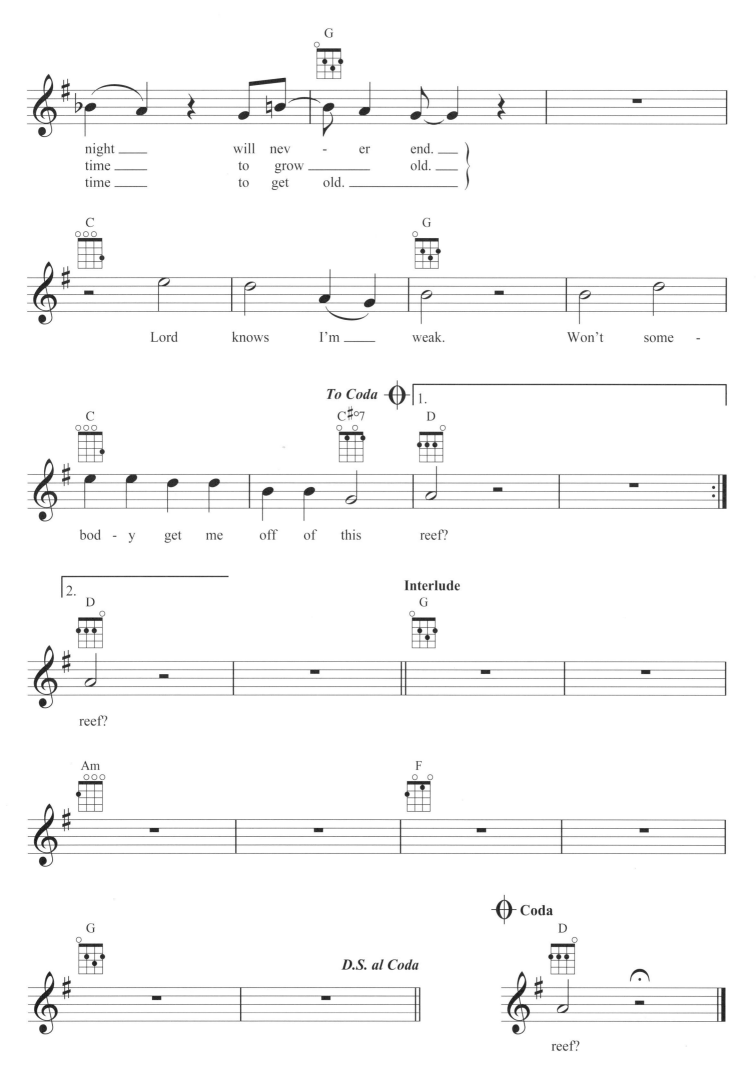

night _____ will nev - er end. _____
time _____ to grow _____ old. _____
time _____ to get old. _____

Lord knows I'm _____ weak. Won't some -

To Coda ⊕ | 1.

bod - y get me off of this reef?

| 2.

reef?

Interlude

D.S. al Coda

⊕ **Coda**

reef?

Boss D.J.

Words and Music by Brad Nowell

Mm, __ mm, mm - hm, __ mm, _____

_____ mm - hm. __ Mm - hm. Don't

Chorus

stop. 'Cause it's so __
It's so __

__ nice. _____ __ I wan - na hear the
__ nice. _____ __ I wan - na hear the

1. same song twice. __ 2. same song twice. **Outro** Now - a - days __ the

songs on the ra - di - o _____ all, all __ drive me cra - zy. __
Let chord ring.

Caress Me Down

Words and Music by Brad Nowell, Eric Wilson and Floyd Gaugh

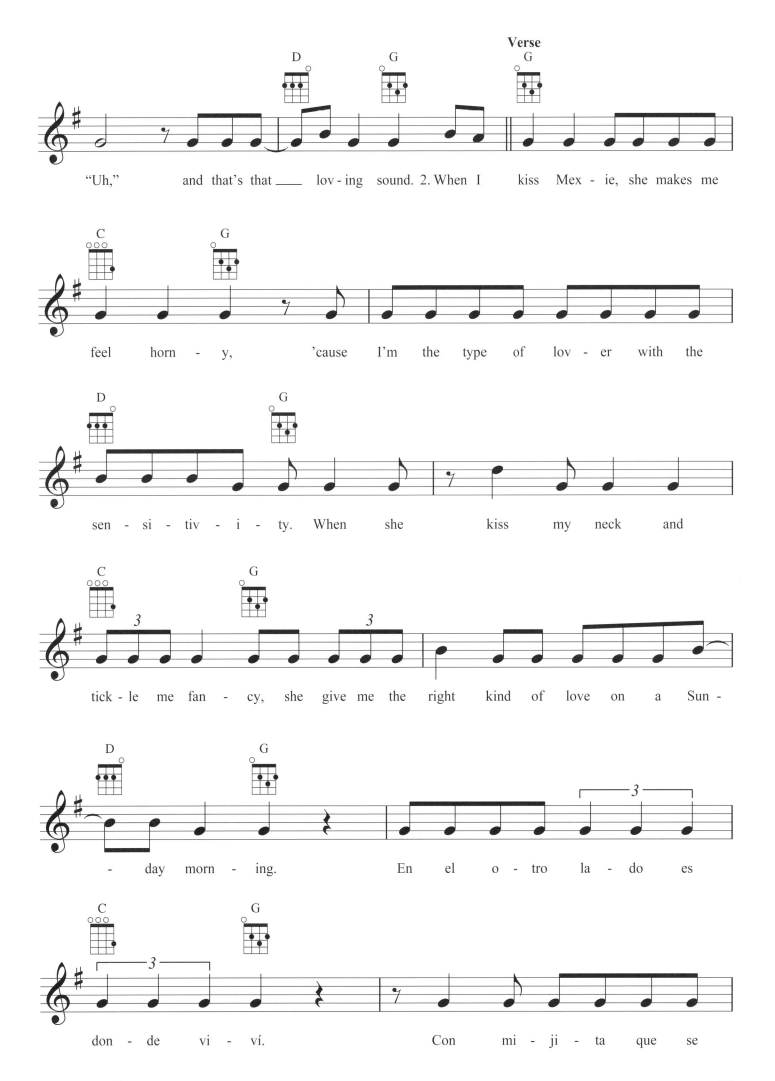

lla - ma Mex - ie. Y su her - ma - na, si ____ me quie - ré.

Y a - ho - ri - ta ten - e - mos un be - bé. Sus pa - dre, sus tios, tra -

ta - ron ma - tar, but they did not get ____ too far. ____ Un

po - co des - pués tu - vé que re - gre - sar con un chin - go de di - ne - ro, 'cause you

know I'm a star. Yo fui a Cos - ta Ri - ca pa - ra to -

mar y sur - fe - ar. Pla - ti - ca - ba con la ra - za, 'cause they

know who we are. Sí no me di - ó cuen - ta, then I bet you nev - er will. You

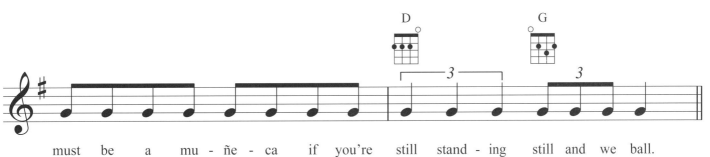

must be a mu - ñe - ca if you're still stand - ing still and we ball.

Chorus

"Uh." And the girl ca - ress me down. "Uh," and that's the ___

___ lov - ing sound. We go, "uh," and the girl ca - ress me down.

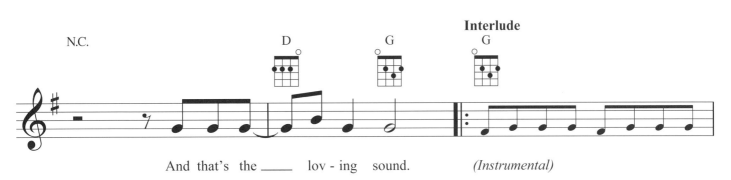

And that's the ___ lov - ing sound. *(Instrumental)*

Play 3 times

Date Rape

Words and Music by Brad Nowell

First note

Verse
Fast

1. Let me tell you 'bout a girl I know. ___

Had a drink a - bout an hour a - go, ___ sit - ting in the cor - ner

by her - self, in a bar in down - town hell.

She heard a noise and she looked through the door, ___

and saw a man she'd nev - er seen be - fore. ___ Light skin,

light blue eyes, __ a dou - ble chin and a plas - tic smile. __ Well,

Her heart raced as he walked in the door __ and took an emp - ty seat next to

her at the bar. __ "My brand - new car is parked right out - side. __

How'd you like to go for a ride?" __ And she said, "Wait a min - ute; I

have to think." __ He said, __ "That's fine; __ may I please buy you a drink?" __

One drink turned in - to three or four, __ and they left and got in - to his car, __

and they drove a-way some-place real far.

Verse

2. "Now, babe, the time has come. __

How'd you like to have a lit-tle fun?" __ And she said, "If we could on-ly

please be on our way, __ I would not run." __

That's when things got out of con-trol.

She did-n't want to. He had his way. She said, "Let's go."

He said, "No way. Come on, ba - by, it's your luck - y day. ___

Shut your mouth; we're gon - na do it my way. ___

Come on, ba - by, don't be a - fraid. ___ If it

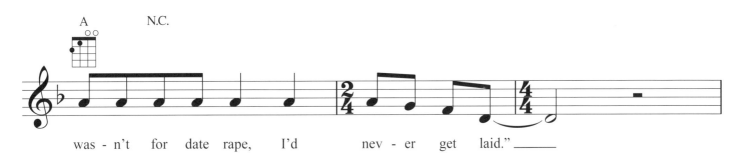

was - n't for date rape, I'd nev - er get laid." _____

Verse

3. He fin - ished up and he start - ed the car. ___

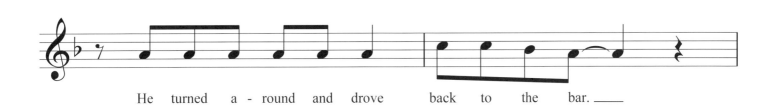

He turned a - round and drove back to the bar. ___

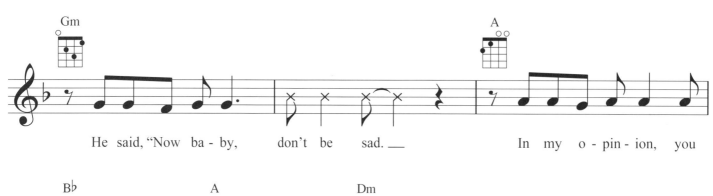

He said, "Now ba - by, don't be sad. __ In my o - pin - ion, you

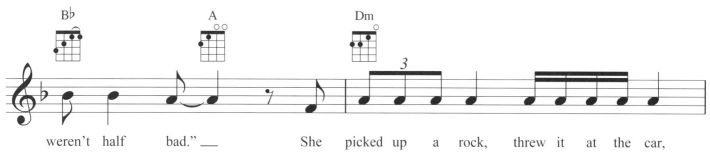

weren't half bad." __ She picked up a rock, threw it at the car,

hit him in the head, and now he's got a big scar. Come

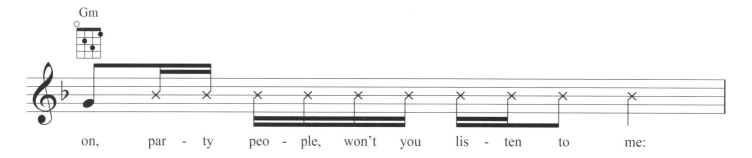

on, par - ty peo - ple, won't you lis - ten to me:

date rape styl - ee. The next day she went to her drawer, __

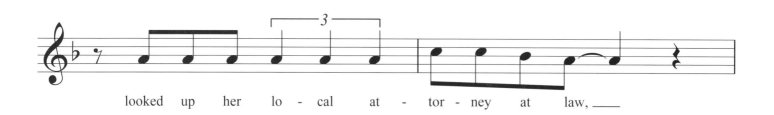

looked up her lo - cal at - tor - ney at law, ___

went to the phone and filed a po - lice re - port, ___

and then she took the guy's ass to court. ___ Well, the day he stood in

front of the judge ___ he screamed, ___ "She lies, ___ that lit - tle slut!" ___

The judge knew he was full of shit, and he gave him twen - ty - five

years. And now his heart is filled with tears. ___

Verse

___ 4. One night in jail, it was get - ting late.

He was butt - raped by a large in - mate, ___ and he screamed, _

___ but the guards paid no at - ten - tion to his

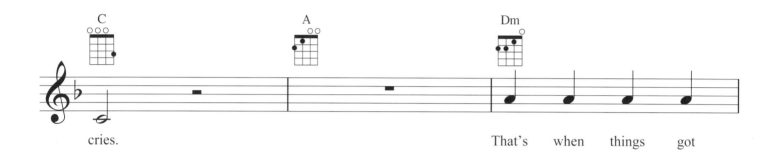

cries. That's when things got

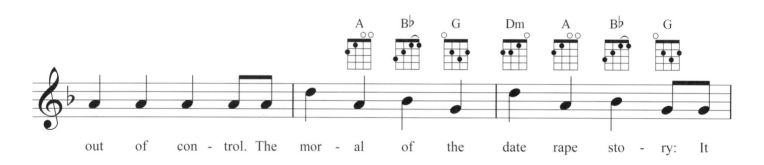

out of con - trol. The mor - al of the date rape sto - ry: It

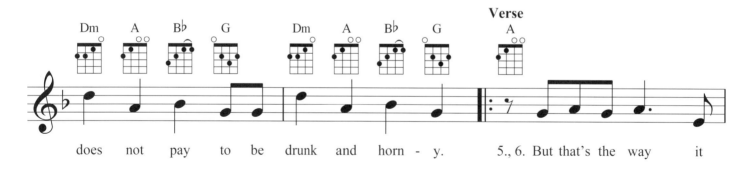

Verse

does not pay to be drunk and horn - y. 5., 6. But that's the way it

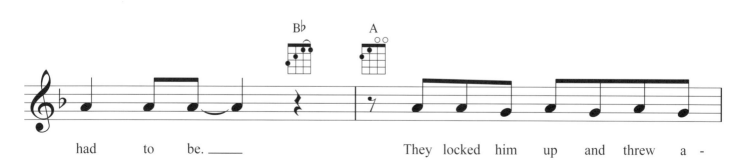

had to be. ___ They locked him up and threw a -

way the key. ___ Well, I can't take pit - y on

men of his kind, ___ e - ven though he now takes it

in the be - hind. ___

in the be - hind. ___ Take a break.

Outro

Ba - na - na - na - na - na, _____ ba -

- na - na - na - na - na. _____

Ba - na - na - na - na - na, _____ la -

- la - la - la - la - la. _____

She did - n't want to, she did - n't want to,

she did - n't want to, she did - n't want to take it.

Don't Push

Words and Music by Brad Nowell

First note

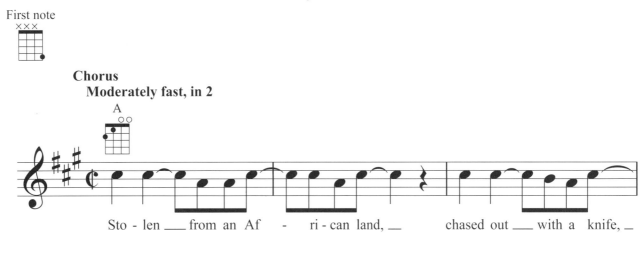

Chorus
Moderately fast, in 2

Sto - len ___ from an Af - ri - can land, ___ chased out ___ with a knife, ___

___ with a face like Bob Mar - ley and a mouth ___ like a mo - tor - bike. ___

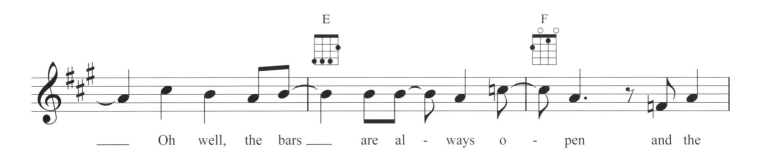

___ Oh well, the bars ___ are al - ways o - pen and the

time is al - ways right. ___ And if God's good word goes un - spo - ken, the

Verse

mu - sic goes all night. And it ___ goes: 1. If I were Bob Mar - ley I'd say,

"Could you be loved?" And if I was Half Pint or with my Lord up a-bove, if I

was Mike Ty-son I would look for a fight, and if I was a Boom-town Rat I would be

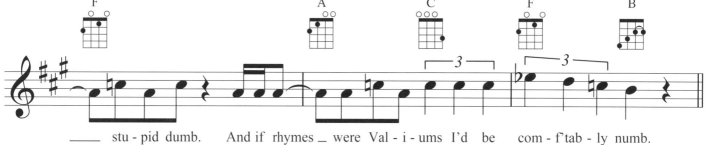

stay-ing up all night. If I was the king Ad - Rock I would get __

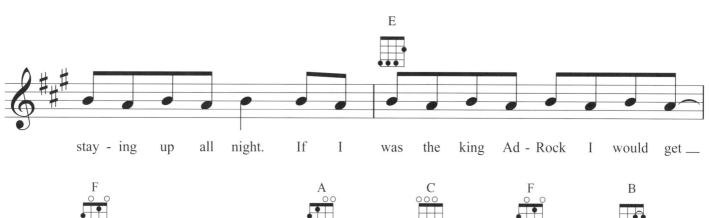

__ stu - pid dumb. And if rhymes __ were Val - i - ums I'd be com - f'tab - ly numb.

Chorus

If I had a shot - gun, you know what I'd do? __ I'd

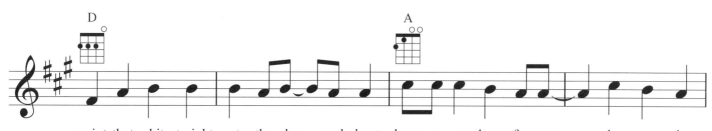

point that shit straight at the sky __ and shoot heav - en on down for you, __ be - cause the

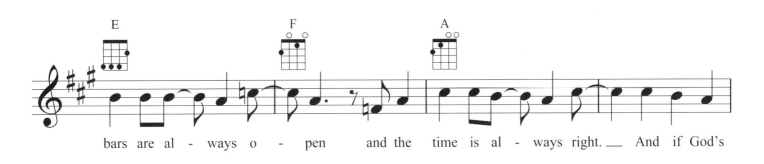

bars are al - ways o - pen and the time is al - ways right. __ And if God's

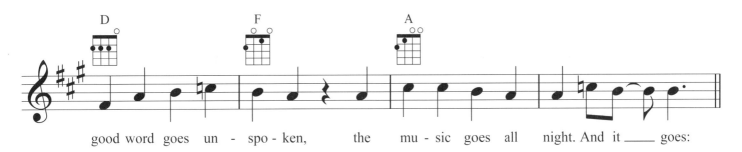

good word goes un - spo - ken, the mu - sic goes all night. And it __ goes:

Verse

2. I want a lov - er, but I can't find the time. I want a rea - son, but I

can't find the rhyme. And I wan - na start some stat - ic, but I can't af - ford __ to

get slammed to the ground like I fall off my skate - board. Hey,

but now - a - days, as clear as you please, get strapped with pro - tec - tion or

Bridge 1

I was chased out of the ___ bar. _____

I saw ___ my best friend to -

night, so don't push me ___ too ___ far. _____

Interlude

1.–3.

4.

2. I'm gon - na

Verse

run, come down with the new lyr - ics. ___ Get hip, get hip, don't slip, ___

___ you knuck - le - heads. Rac - is - m is schis - m on a se - ri - ous tip. You don't be -

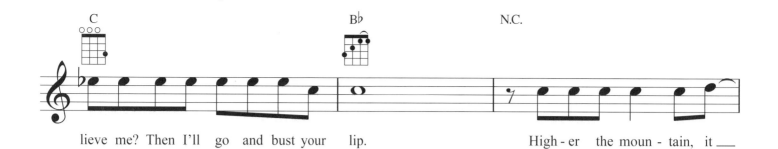

lieve me? Then I'll go and bust your lip. High-er the moun-tain, it ___

___ hard to climb. Rough-er the rhy-thm, then it must be Sub-lime.

Lis-ten, yel-low lov-er, yeah, they're right on time. We got crick-et with the quick-ness and the

Interlude

bass line.

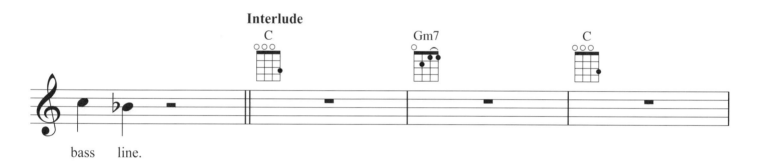

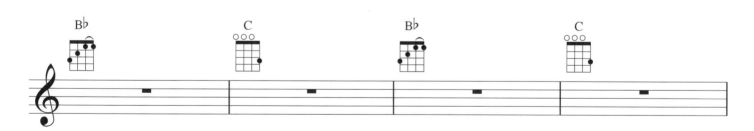

Bridge 3

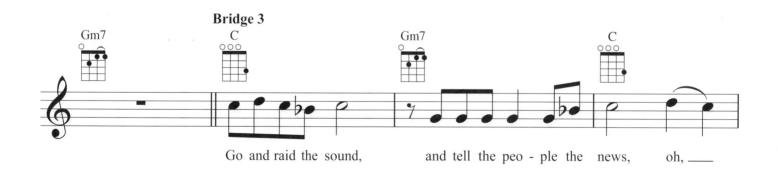

Go and raid the sound, and tell the peo-ple the news, oh, ___

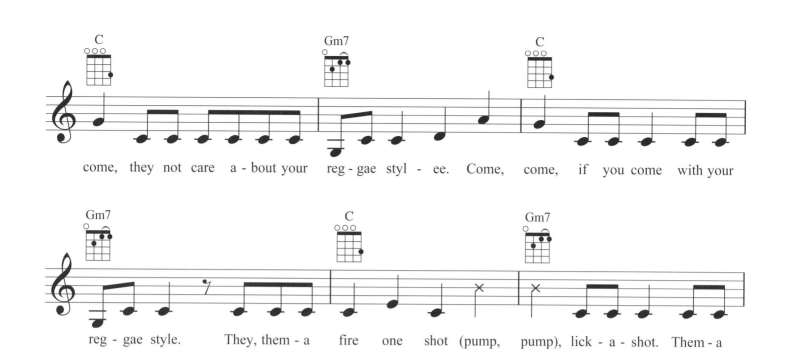

come, they not care a - bout your reg - gae styl - ee. Come, come, if you come with your

reg - gae style. They, them - a fire one shot (pump, pump), lick - a - shot. Them - a

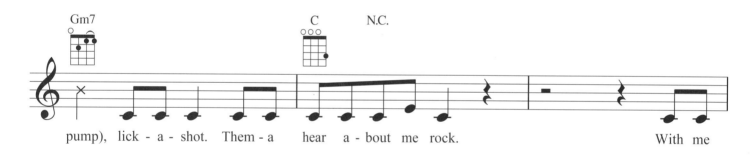

fire two shot (pump, pump), lick - a - shot. Them - a fire three shot (pump,

pump), lick - a - shot. Them - a hear a - bout me rock. With me

ar - mor, do a launch, then at - tack me with their ar - mor. Me no stop.

Coun - ter - re - act - ing with their ar - mor. Fear who are launch, them at - tack me with their

ar - mor. Me no stop. Coun - ter - re - act - ing, them big - ger. Hear me cop - y,

Interlude

Play 4 times

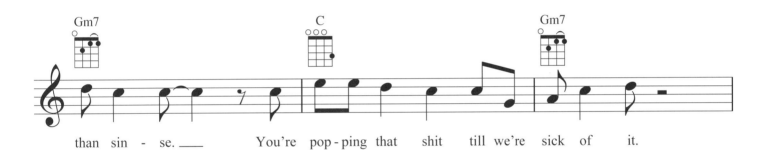

tell you 'bout this reg - gae styl - ee.

Outro

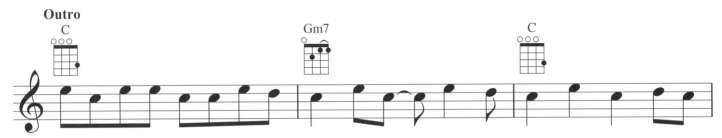

Peo - ple wan - na come up and they want tell me ___ smok - ing crack co - caine bet - ter

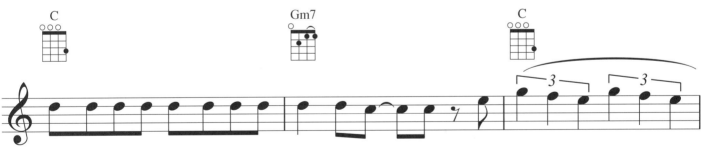

than sin - se. ___ You're pop - ping that shit till we're sick of it.

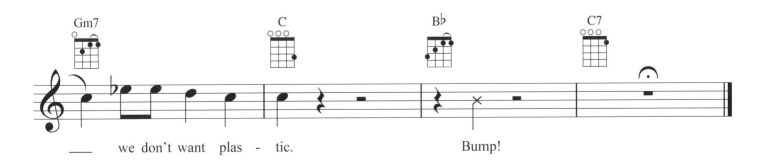

Tweak - ing ev - 'ry week - end and we just can't take ___ it. Ooh, whoa, ___

___ we don't want plas - tic. Bump!

Doin' Time

Words and Music by Brad Nowell, Adam Horovitz, Adam Yauch, Rick Rubin, Marshall Goodman, George Gershwin, Ira Gershwin, DuBose Heyward and Dorothy Heyward

First note

Chorus
Moderately, in 2

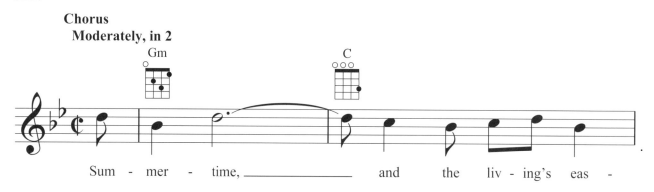

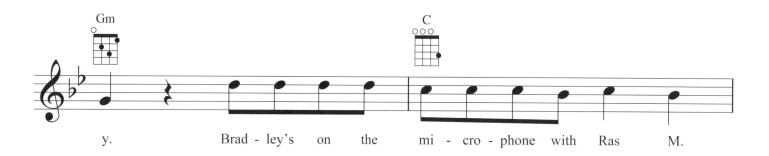

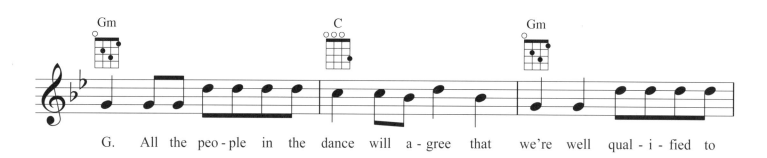

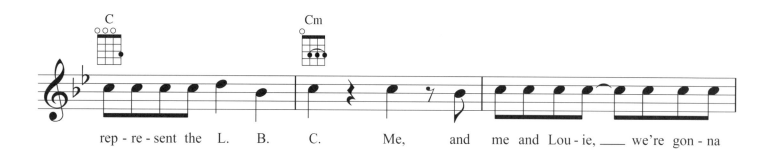

run to the par - ty and dance __ to the rhy - thm, it gets __ hard - er. __

Verse

1. Me and my girl, __

__ we got this re - la - tion - ship. __

I love her so bad, _____ but she treats me like shit.

On lock - down, like a pen - i - ten - tia - ry. __

__ She spreads her lov - ing all o - ver, and when __

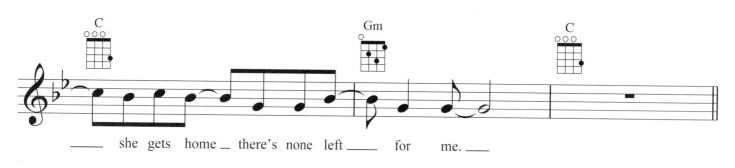

_____ she gets home _ there's none left _____ for me. _____

𝄋 Chorus

Sum - mer - time, _____ and the liv-ing's eas - y. Brad - ley's on the

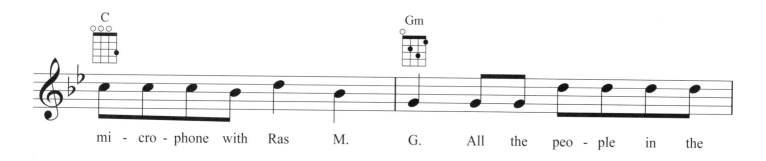

mi - cro - phone with Ras M. G. All the peo - ple in the

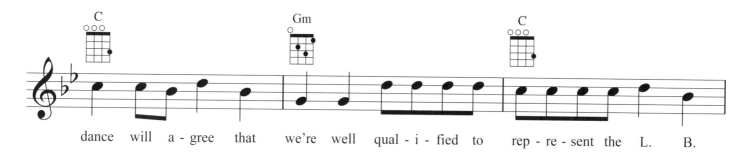

dance will a - gree that we're well qual - i - fied to rep - re - sent the L. B.

C. Me, and me and Lou - ie, _____ we're gon - na run to the par - ty and dance _

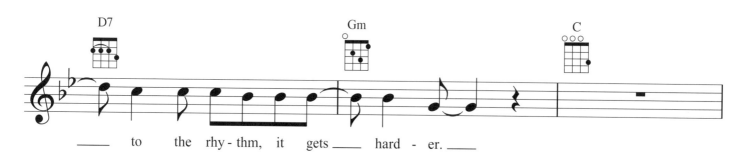

_____ to the rhy - thm, it gets _____ hard - er. _____

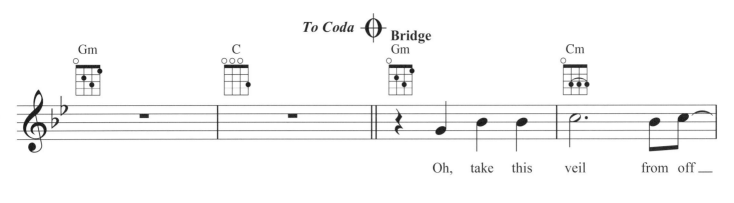

Oh, take this veil from off __

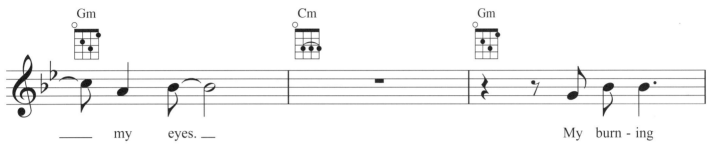

__ my eyes. __

My burn - ing

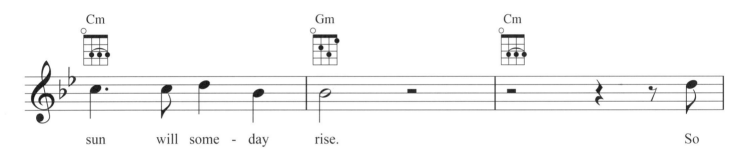

sun will some - day rise.

So

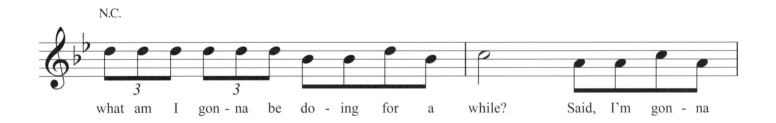

what am I gon - na be do - ing for a while? Said, I'm gon - na

play with my - self. __

Show them __ now

we've come off the shelf. _____

So what?

Brad-ley's on the mi-cro-phone with Ras M. G. All the peo-ple in the

dance will a-gree that we're ___ well qual-i-fied to rep-re-sent the L. B.

C. Me, la-la, Lou-ie, well, ev-'ry-bod-y

run to the rhy-thm, it gets hard-er, hard-er.

Sum-mer-time, ___ and the liv-ing's eas-

y.

Garden Grove

Words and Music by Brad Nowell, Eric Wilson, Floyd Gaugh and Linton Johnson

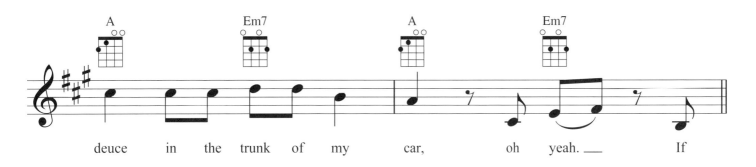

deuce in the trunk of my car, oh yeah. __ If

Pre-Chorus

you on - ly knew all the love that I've found, __ it's

hard to keep my soul on the ground. You're a

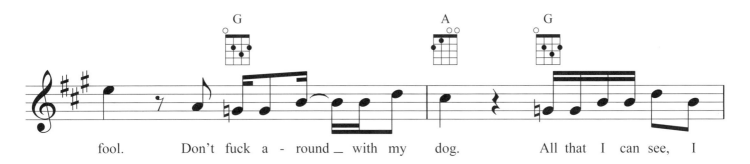

fool. Don't fuck a - round __ with my dog. All that I can see, I

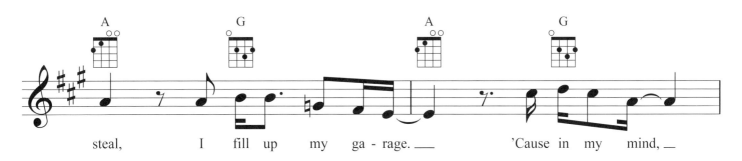

steal, I fill up my ga - rage. __ 'Cause in my mind, __

mu - sic from Ja - mai - ca, all the love that I've found... __ Pull

o - ver, there's a rea - son why my soul's __ un - sound: __ it's

Chorus

you. It's that shit stuck un - der my shoe. It's that smell in - side the van. __

__ It's my bed - sheet cov - ered with sand. Sit - ting through a shit - ty

band. Get - ting dog shit on my hand. Get - ting has - sled by the

man. Wak - ing up to an a - larm. Stick - ing nee - dles in your

arm. Pick - ing up trash on a free - way. Feel - ing de - pressed ev - er - y

day. Leav - ing with - out mak - ing a sound. Pick - ing my dog up at the

pound. Liv - ing in a tweak - er pad. Get - ting yelled at by my

dad. Say - ing I'm hap - py when I'm not. Find - ing roach - es in the

Outro

pot. Oh, _____ all these things I do, __

__ they're wait - ing for

you.

Jailhouse

Words and Music by Brad Nowell, Eric Wilson and Floyd Gaugh

Chorus

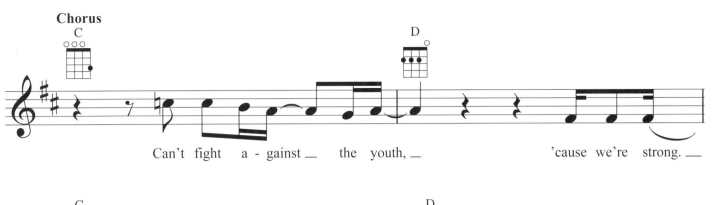

Can't fight a - gainst __ the youth, __ 'cause we're strong. __

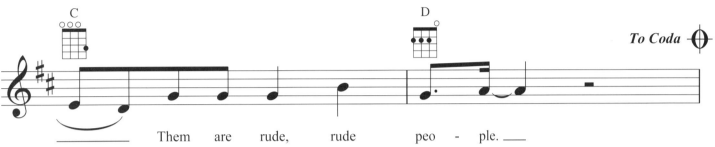

__ Them are rude, rude peo - ple. __

To Coda ⊕

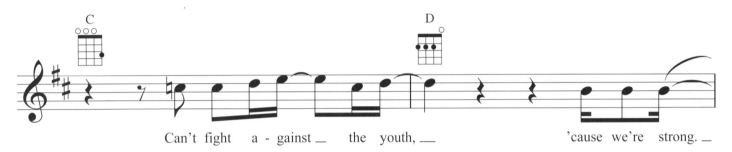

Can't fight a - gainst __ the youth, __ 'cause we're strong. __

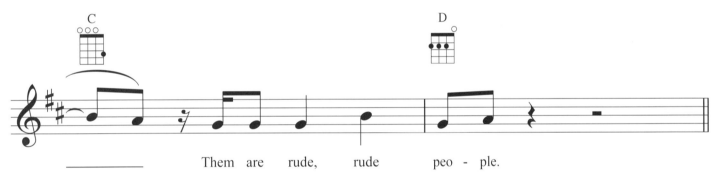

__ Them are rude, rude peo - ple.

Verse

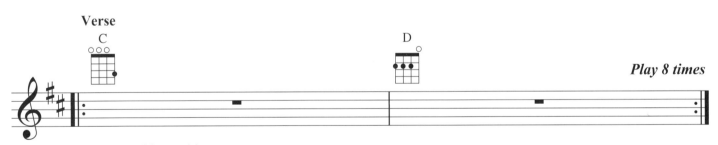

Play 8 times

2. *See additional lyrics*

Interlude

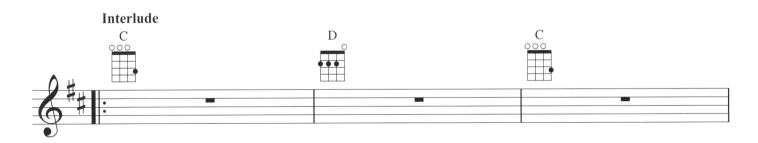

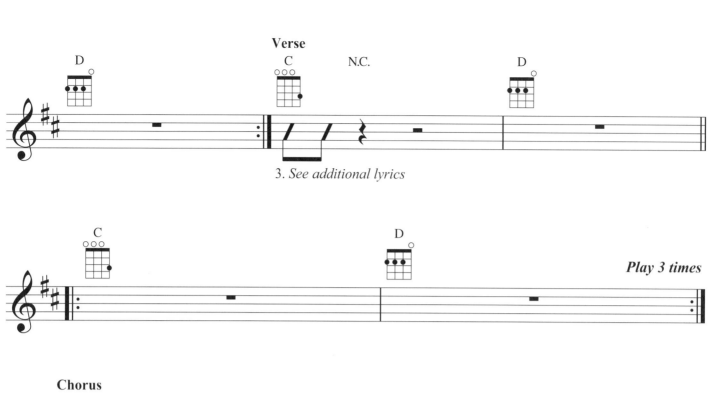

3. *See additional lyrics*

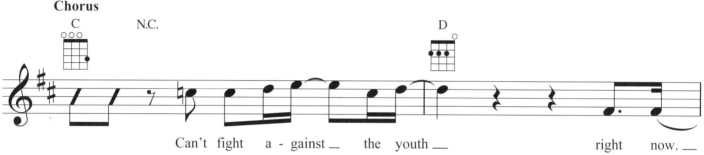

Play 3 times

Chorus

Can't fight a - gainst __ the youth __ right now. __

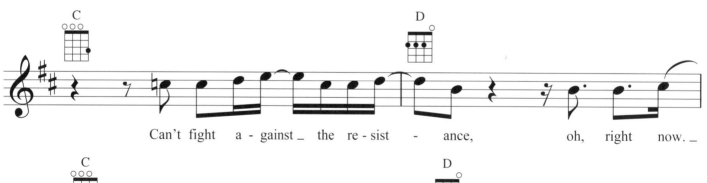

__ Them are rude, rude peo - ple.

Can't fight a - gainst __ the re - sist - ance, oh, right now. __

__ Them are rude, rude peo - ple.

Verse

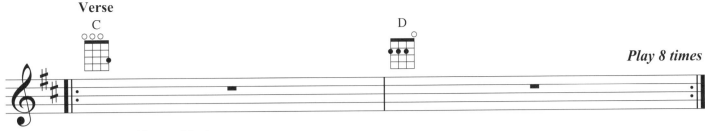

Play 8 times

4. *See additional lyrics*

Interlude

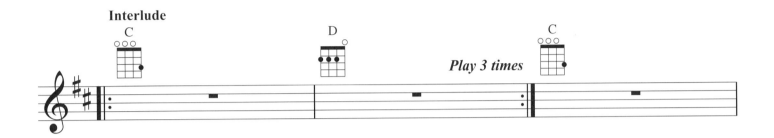

Play 3 times

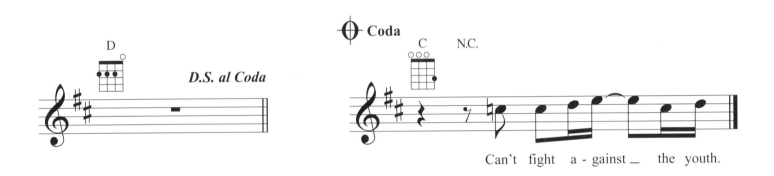

D.S. al Coda

Coda

Can't fight a - gainst the youth.

Additional Lyrics

2. When I was a youth in 1983, was the best day of my life. Had the '89 vision.
   We didn't fuss or no fight when all the little daughters wanna be my wife.
   Like a vision, it was playin' on my guitar, on my guitar. I had to be there, I had to be there.
   I had to be there, I had to be there. When the rhythm was playin', I know that I'm gonna be there, yeah.
   Oh, Bud Gaugh will be singing there and Eric Wilson will be banging out there, yeah.
   Oh, and we'll be all singin' with versions, with versions. Reggae version, version, version, version. Oh.

3. What has been told to the wise and uprooted, yeah, it's gonna be revealed unto babes and Sublime. *(Ad lib.)*

4. We gonna rule this land. Come on, children, we gonna rule this land.
   'Cause when that rhythm, it was playin' on my guitar, on my guitar, I had to be there, I had to be there.
   I had to be there, I had to be there. Oh, when I was a youth it was the best day, it was the best day of my life.
   We had the '89 vision. We didn't fuss or no fight when all the little daughters wanna be my wife.
   When that rhythm, it was playin' on my guitar, on my guitar, I had to be there, I had to be there.
   I had to be there, I had to be there. I had to be there, I had to be there. Had to be there.

Let's Go Get Stoned

Words and Music by Brad Nowell

First note

Intro
Moderately

I swear some-times you're tak-ing me ___ for grant-

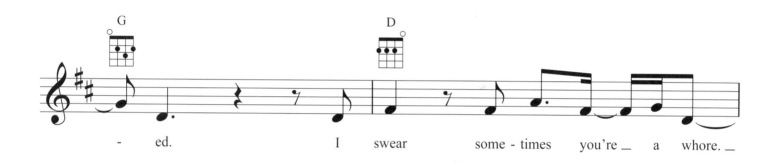

-ed. I swear some-times you're ___ a whore. ___

___ I swear, but I know there ain't ___ no rea-

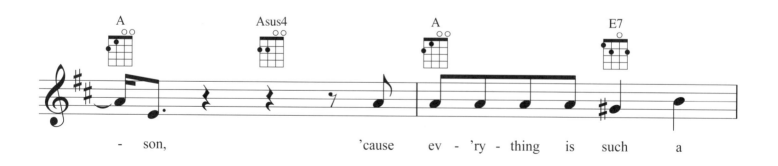

-son, 'cause ev-'ry-thing is such a

bore.   1. At night I had __ a dream, ___

though it made __ me sick. __ Saw you in ___ your bed - room suck - ing

some - one el - se's dick. __ (My good-ness.) My friends all laughed, __

said it was ___ my fault. Said it's time that it hap - pened to

me.   But I know that the show was

much more than a blow, __ so I'm wait - in' for the tide to get

low,   wait - in' for the tide to get

Verse

low.   2. If I was an ant ___ crawl -

in' up - on ___ the wall, ___   tell me, ba - by, would it

make no dif - f'rence ___ at all? _____   If I was a

roach   on   a   tree,   tell   me,   would   you   smoke

me, ___   mm? _____   Bright   lights ___

Same in the End

Words and Music by Brad Nowell, Eric Wilson and Floyd Gaugh

1. Down in Mis - sis - sip - pi where the sun beats down from the sky,

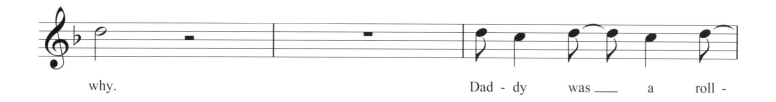

they give it up and they give it up and they give it up, but they nev - er ask

why. Dad - dy was ___ a roll -

- in', roll - in' stone, ___ oh. ___ He

rolled a - way ___ one day ___ and he nev - er came home.

to be - lieve __ when you light ___ up in the back with those tricks _

__ up your sleeve. _ That don't mean _ I ___ can't hang. _ 2. The day _

that I die __ will be the day that I shut my mouth and

put down my gui - tar. ____ Sun - day morn - ing hold
fied ass son of a bitch. _ Rec - tite on my

church down at the bar. ___ Get down on your
ass and it makes me itch. ___ I can see for

knees and __ start to pray, __ oh. _____
miles and __ miles and miles, __ oh. _____

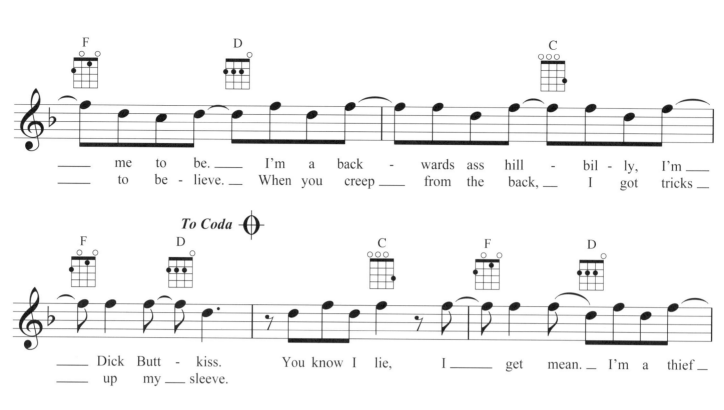

_____ me to be. _____ I'm a back - wards ass hill - bil - ly, I'm _____
_____ to be - lieve. _____ When you creep _____ from the back, _____ I got tricks _____

To Coda

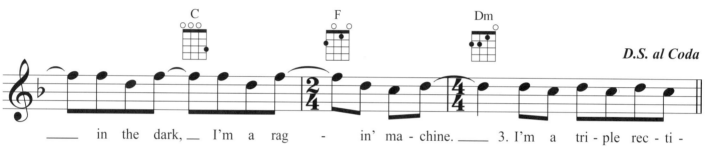

_____ Dick Butt - kiss. You know I lie, I _____ get mean. _ I'm a thief _
_____ up my _____ sleeve.

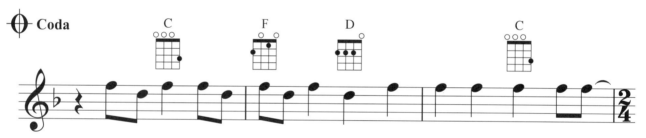

D.S. al Coda

_____ in the dark, _ I'm a rag - in' ma - chine. _____ 3. I'm a tri - ple rec - ti -

Coda

_____ Twen - ty-four sev - en, dev-il's best friend, makes no dif - f'rence, it's all _

Outro

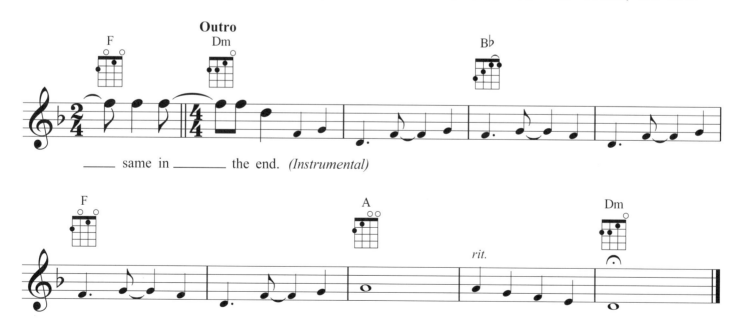

_____ same in _____ the end. _(Instrumental)_

rit.

Smoke Two Joints

Words and Music by Chris Kay and Michael Kay

Verse

2. Dad - dy, he once told __ me, "Son, __ you be hard - work - ing man." __ And

Mom - ma, she once told __ me, "Son, __ you do the best __ you can." But

then one day __ I met a man __ who came to me __ and said, ___

"Hard work good and hard work fine, but first take care of head." ___

Interlude

Play 4 times

Whoa.

Outro

Rock me to - night _____ for _ old times' sake. _

Whoa. _____

Santeria

Words and Music by Brad Nowell, Eric Wilson and Floyd Gaugh

all I real-ly wan-na say _____ I can't de-fine. _____

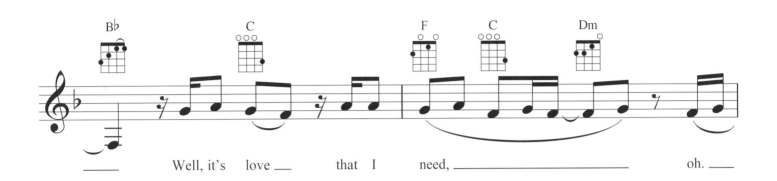

_____ Well, it's love _____ that I need, _____ oh. _____

𝄋 **Verse**

_____ 2. My soul will have _____ to wait 'til I _____ get back, find a
3. *See additional lyrics*

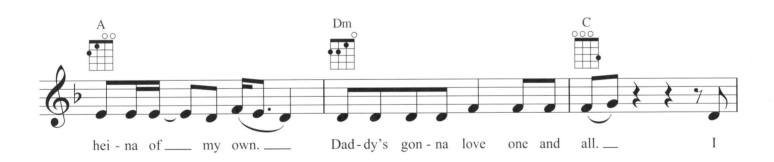

hei-na of _____ my own. _____ Dad-dy's gon-na love one and all. _____ I

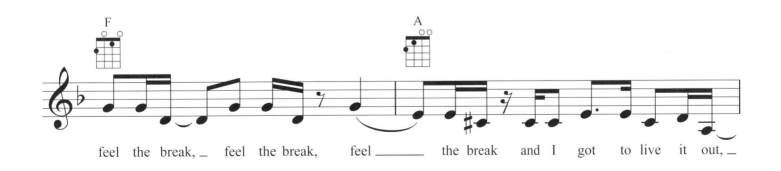

feel the break, _____ feel the break, feel _____ the break and I got to live it out, _____

oh, ___ yeah, huh. Well, I swear that I, _____

Chorus

___ well, I real-ly wan-na know, ___ ah, ba-by,
(See additional chorus lyrics)

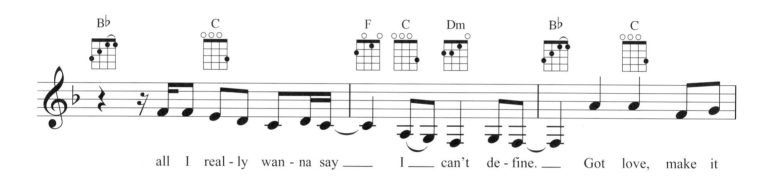

all I real-ly wan-na say _____ I ___ can't de-fine. ___ Got love, make it

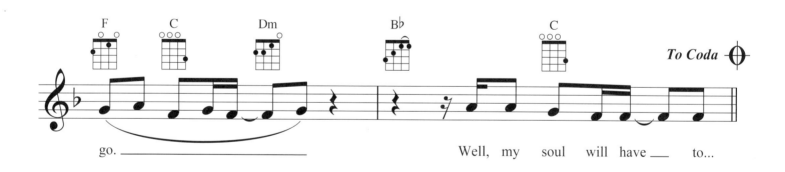

go. _____ Well, my soul will have ___ to...

Interlude

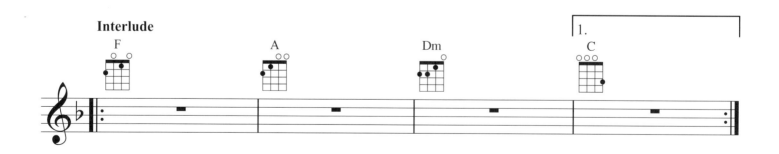

74

Additional Lyrics

3. Tell sanchito that if he knows what is good for him, he best go run and hide.
   Daddy's got a new forty-five,
   And I won't think twice to stick that barrel straight down sancho's throat.
   Believe me when I say that I got something for his punk ass.

Chorus: What I really want to know, ah, baby,
   Ooh, what I really wanna say is there's just one
   Way back, and I'll make it, yeah.
   My soul will have to wait.

Scarlet Begonias

Words by Robert Hunter
Music by Jerry Garcia

First note

Verse
Reggae Rock

1. As I was walk - ing down Gros - ve - nor Square,   not a
(2.) rings on her fin - gers and bells on her shoes,   and I

chill to the weath - er, but a nip to the air.
knew with - out ask - ing, she was in - to the blues.

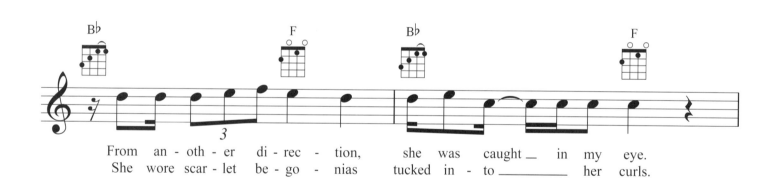

From an - oth - er di - rec - tion, she was caught __ in my eye.
She wore scar - let be - go - nias tucked in - to _____ her curls.

It could be __ an il - lu - sion, but I might __ as well try, might as well
I knew right __ a - way she was not like oth - er girls, like oth - er

try.
girls.

1.

2. She had

Well, I ain't

Bridge 1

nev - er been right, ___ as I ain't nev - er been wrong. It

sel - dom works out ___ the way it does in this song.

Hey!   'Cause once in a while, _ you get shown _ in the light _ in the strang-

- est of plac - es if you look at it right.

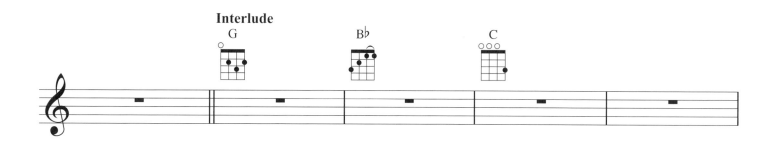

Interlude

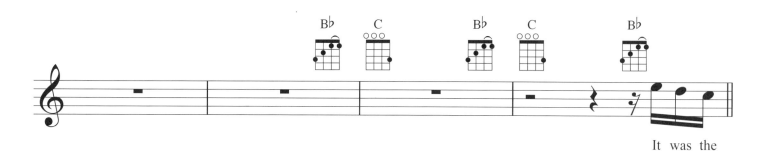

It was the

Bridge 2

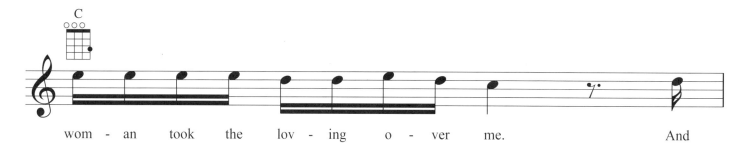

sum - mer of love ___ and I thank the stars a - bove be - cause the

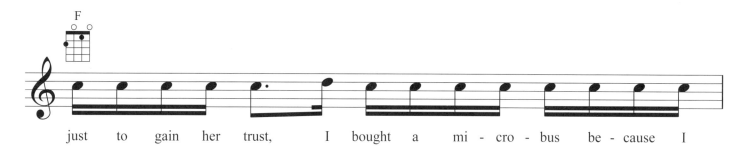

wom - an took the lov - ing o - ver me. And

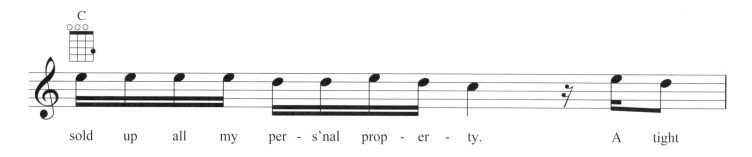

just to gain her trust, I bought a mi - cro - bus be - cause I

sold up all my per - s'nal prop - er - ty. A tight

tie - dyed dress, she was a psy-che-del-ic mess. We toured to the north, south, east and west. We

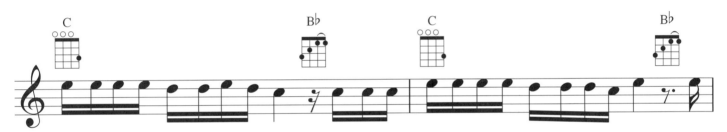

sold some mush-room tea, we sold some ec-sta-sy, we sold

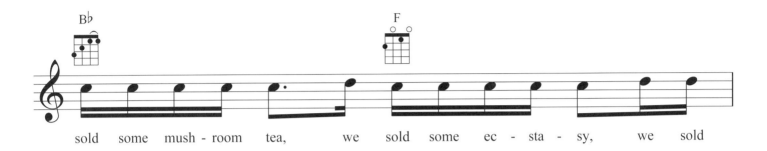

ni - trous, o - pium, ac - id, her - o - in and P. C. P. and now I

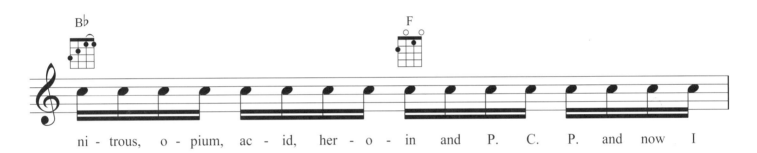

hear the po-lice com-ing af-ter me. Yes, now I hear the po-lice com-ing af-ter me. The

one Scar-let, with the flow-ers in her hair, she's got the

po-lice com-ing af-ter me. 3. Well, there ain't __

80

Wrong Way

Words and Music by Brad Nowell, Eric Wilson and Floyd Gaugh

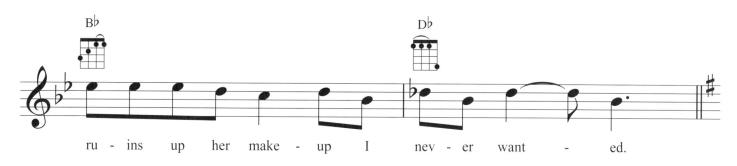

ru – ins up her make - up I nev - er want - ed.

Verse

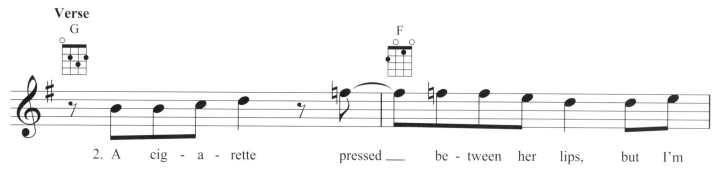

2. A cig - a - rette pressed ___ be - tween her lips, but I'm

star - ing at her tits, it's the wrong way. ___ Strong if I can, but I

am on - ly a man. So I take her to the can, it's the wrong way. ___

Bridge 1

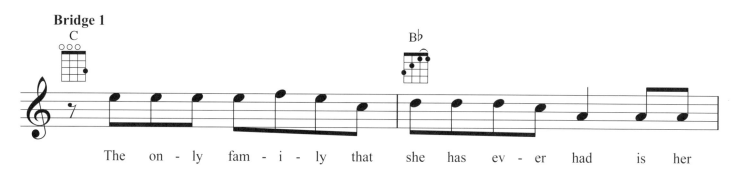

The on - ly fam - i - ly that she has ev - er had is her

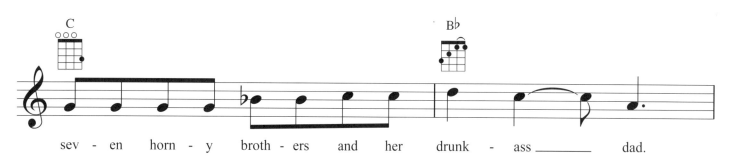

sev - en horn - y broth - ers and her drunk - ass ___ dad.

He need-ed mon-ey, so he put her on the street. Ev-'ry-

thing was go-ing fine un-til the day she met _____ me.

Verse

3. Hap-py, are you sad, wan - na shoot your dad? I'll do

an-y-thing I can, the wrong way. __ We talk all night, tried __

__ to make it right. Be-lieve me, shit was tight, it was the

Bridge 2

wrong way. __ Don't run a-way if you want to stay, __ 'cause I

ain't here to make you, oh, — no. It's up to you, what you

real-ly want to do. Spend some time in A-mer-i-ca. Ha, dub — style!

Interlude

Trombone solo - ad lib.

2.

Chorus

Solo ends She'll give you all that she's got to give, — but

I'm gon-na make it hard to live. — Big, salt-y tears roll-ing

down to her chin, and it smears up her make-up I nev-er want - ed.

What I Got

Words and Music by Brad Nowell, Eric Wilson, Floyd Gaugh and Lindon Roberts

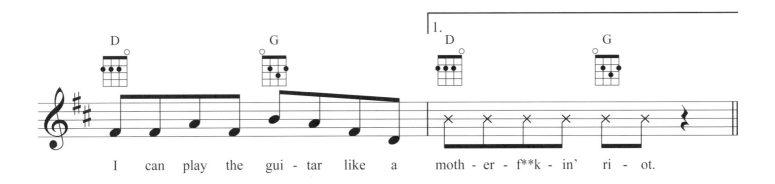

I can play the gui - tar like a moth - er - f**k - in' ri - ot.

Interlude

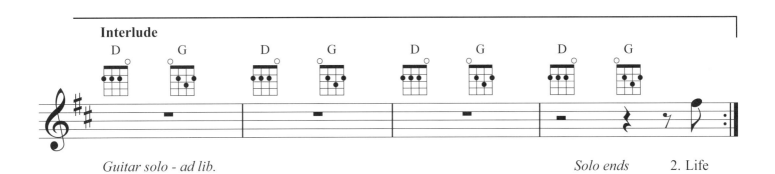

Guitar solo - ad lib.   *Solo ends*   2. Life

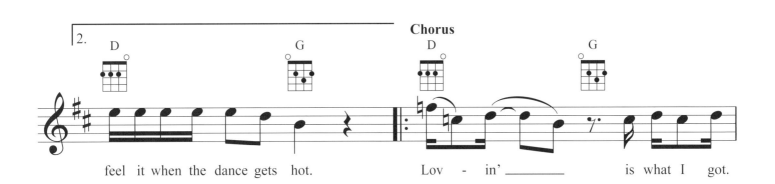

feel it when the dance gets hot.   Lov - in' _____ is what I got.

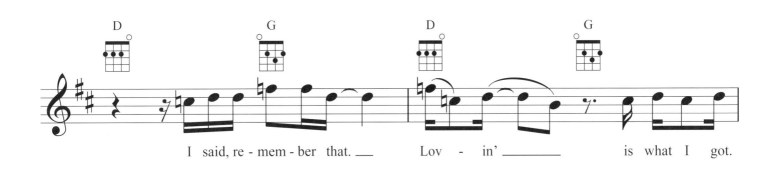

I said, re - mem - ber that. __   Lov - in' _____ is what I got.

Re - mem - ber that. __

D.C. al Coda

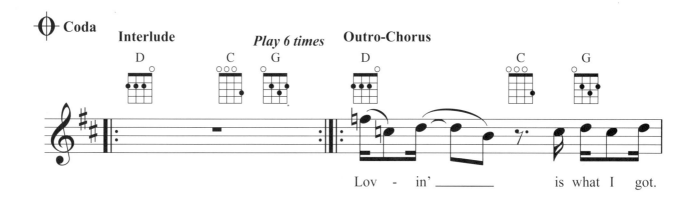

Lov - in' _____ is what I got.

I said, re - mem - ber that. ___ Lov - in' _____ is what I got, _

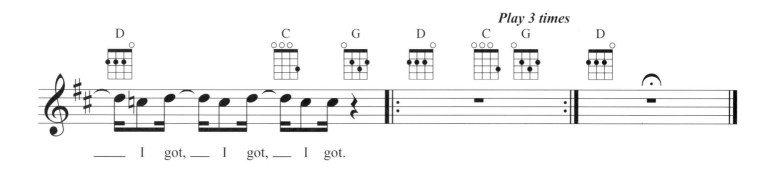

___ I got, ___ I got, ___ I got.

Additional Lyrics

2. Life is (too short), so love the one you got,
   'Cause you might get run over or you might get shot.
   Never start no static, I just get it off my chest.
   Never had to battle with no bulletproof vest.
   Take a small example, take a t-t-t-tip from me:
   Take all of your money, give it all to charity.
   Love is what I got, it's within my reach,
   And the Sublime style's still straight from Long Beach.
   It all comes back to you, you finally get what you deserve.
   Try and test that, you're bound to get served.
   Love's what I got, don't start a riot.
   You'll feel it when the dance gets hot.

3. I don't cry when my dog runs away.
   I don't get angry at the bills I have to pay.
   I don't get angry when my mom smokes pot,
   Hits the bottle and moves right to the rock.
   F**kin' and fightin', it's all the same.
   Livin' with Louie Dog's the only way to stay sane.
   Let the lovin', let the lovin' come back to me. *(To Coda)*